FISH OUT OF SCHOOL

FISH OUT OF SCHOOL

A Science I CAN READ Book

BY EVELYN SHAW

PICTURES BY RALPH CARPENTIER

Harper & Row, Publishers
New York, Evanston, and London

To Bill Knight, Jr.

FISH OUT OF SCHOOL

The sun had set.

It was night.

In the sea, the herring fish

swam very slowly.

They swam in a group called a school.

Soon the fish stopped swimming
because it was very dark.
They rested together
on the sandy bottom of the sea.
They slept.
Fish do not sleep like people.

They do not have eyelids,

so they cannot close their eyes.

When they sleep,

they seem to be looking

at one another.

The herring fish slept all night.

The sun rose,

and light came into the sea.

One by one

the fish woke up.

They began to move around.

The herring fish formed

into a school.

Together, they swam away

from the sandy bottom.

But one of the herring fish

was still asleep.

When she woke up,

the school was gone.

She looked to her right.

She looked to her left.

She was alone.

All her life, she had lived

with other herring fish.

They had found one another

after they were hatched.

They were less than

a half-inch long.

Now the little fish was one year old.

She was four inches long.

All the fish in the school

looked like her.

They were the same kind, or species.

They were about

the same age and size.

The little herring was not safe
without her school.

She started to look for it.

She swam fast,

up and down

and from side to side.

She could not find

the school anywhere.

And she was hungry.

The school often went

to a coral reef

to search for food.

The little fish swam

toward the coral reef.

Her tail swung right and left.

She was tired and very hungry.

She saw tiny animals and plants

called plankton.

They floated in the water.

She opened her mouth

and ate some plankton.

She circled around

and swallowed more plankton.

Soon she was no longer hungry.

She swam faster toward the coral reef.

Through the clear blue water

she saw sea fans and corals.

She saw animals
that looked like threads.
They moved back and forth
in the water.
She saw dark animals
with long black spines.
These were sea urchins.

A moray eel

stuck its head out of the hole

where it lived.

It had sharp white teeth.

Many kinds of fish

darted in and out

of the little holes in the reef.

They were red, blue, yellow, black.

The reef looked like a flower garden.

One small purple fish

had horns on its head.

25

These fish were not from her school.

They were not her color.

They did not smell like
her school fish.

They did not move like
her school fish.

The little fish swam on.

She poked her head into open spaces
in the coral reef.

She swam toward a bluish fish
with dark stripes.

The fish was called a sergeant major.

He was guarding eggs.

The sergeant major kept other fish

from eating them.

When the little herring fish

swam near,

the sergeant major swam angrily

toward her.

She quickly swam away.

She almost swam into an octopus.

The octopus was sitting under a rock.

He raised three of his eight arms.

But the octopus was too slow.

The little fish got away.

A crab was looking for food
near the rock.

Suddenly the octopus
shot out his arms.

He caught the crab.

He was going to eat it.

The herring fish swam on.

She saw a big dark animal

in the distance.

From far away,

a school of fish

looks like a big dark animal.

It may scare big hungry fish away.

When the little fish

started to swim away,

she saw it was a school.

But the school was in danger.

A sea turtle was chasing the school.

The turtle stretched out his neck.

He snapped at the fish.

He was trying to catch one of them.

But each time he stuck out his head,
the fish changed direction.

The fish in the school

were swimming in many directions.

They looked like small bright flashes.

The turtle could not

catch any fish.

The turtle dived down

to catch a fish.

The school swam up.

The fish got away.

The little herring fish watched them.

She saw that they were different

from the fish that she lived with.

They were blue.

They were larger.

She did not try to join them.

She kept on swimming.

She swam back to the reef.

This time she went to the other side.

The plants that grew there

looked like grass.

Another fish school was feeding

on the sandy bottom.

She went near it.

Suddenly she stopped.

There was something

on the other side of the school.

38

It was a barracuda.

The barracuda was still.

It looked like a log

floating in the water.

The little fish moved

behind the grass.

The barracuda

opened and closed its mouth slowly.

Its teeth stuck out from its jaw.

Suddenly the barracuda
swam into the school.

41

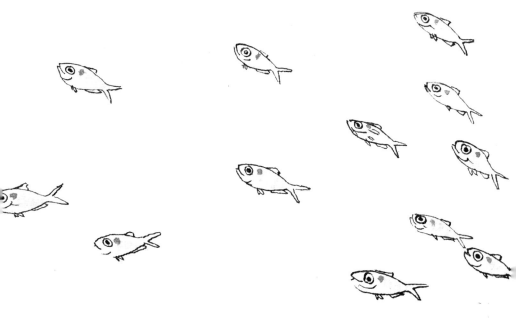

All the fish were frightened.

They swam in many directions.

One fish swam

in front of the barracuda.

The barracuda opened its mouth

and shut its jaws tight.

It ate the fish.

The school swam away.

They swam past the grass

where the little herring fish

was hiding.

These fish looked

just like her school fish.

They were silver with red dots
on their heads.
They were the same size she was.

At last she had found

a school of herring fish.

She swam into it.

There were fish on each side of her.

There were fish above her,

below her, and behind her.

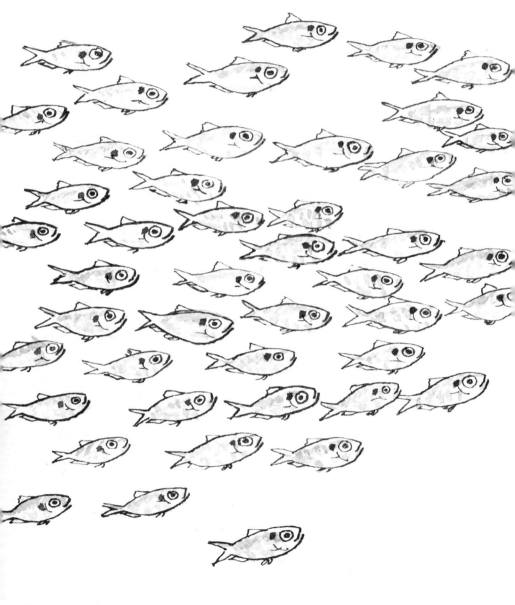

No fish went too far away

from any other fish.

No fish came too close

to any other fish.

She knew she was in the right place.

It was good to be in a school again.

The school of fish looked like
soldiers marching together.
They were all swimming
in the same direction.
They were all swimming
at about the same speed.
They seemed to be playing
follow-the-leader.
In a fish school
any fish can be the leaders.

If the school turns right,
the fish on the right side
become leaders.

If the school turns left,

the fish on the left side

become leaders.

Sometimes the school turns around.

It swims back the way it came.

Then the fish at the back

become the leaders.

The fish turn different ways
to look for food.
When the school found some plankton,
they began to feed.

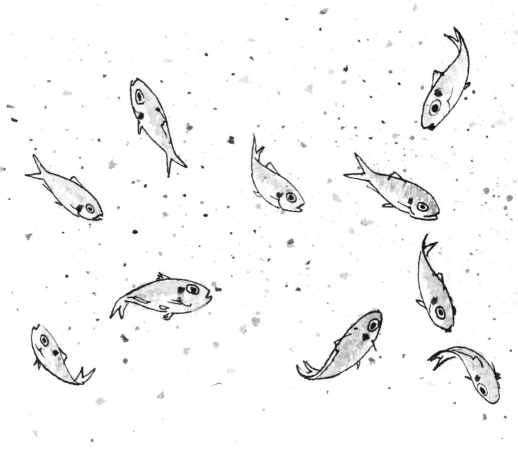

While they fed,

the fish did not swim in a school.

But they never went very far

from each other.

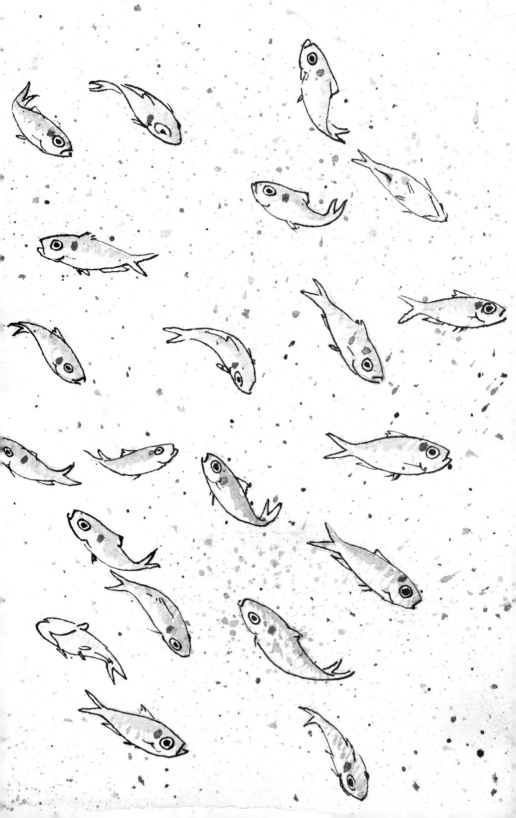

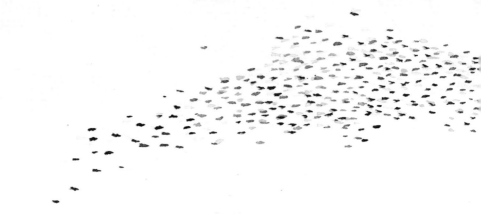

When they finished feeding,

they came close together.

They formed into a school again.

They swam in one direction together.

This was not the same school

that had left the little fish.

She did not know that.

It did not matter.

They were the same kind of fish.

It did not matter

to the school either.

The little fish

looked exactly like them.

The school spent the day

swimming and resting.

In the evening

they searched for food again.

Then night came.

It grew dark in the sea.

The fish became quiet.

With their eyes open,

they went to sleep.

And so did the little fish.

Dr. Evelyn Shaw is a curator in the Department of Animal Behavior at The American Museum of Natural History in New York City.

Dr. Shaw has studied the behavior of fish for fifteen years. She has watched many kinds of fish under water in the Atlantic, in the Pacific, in the Caribbean, and in the Mediterranean.

She wants to find out why some kinds of fish form schools and others do not.

The herring in this book is *Harengula humeralis,* a species which is found in the Caribbean Sea.